Memories of **BARNARD CASTLE**

COUNTY DURHAM BOOKS

Front cover: Modern photograph of the Buttermarket/Market Cross looking towards the Market Place.

Published by County Durham Books, 2007

County Durham Books is the imprint of Durham County Council

ISBN 1897585918

Memories of **BARNARD CASTLE**

Much has changed in Barnard Castle over the years. Did you know for example that the town once had a railway station? It stood on the site of the current GlaxoSmithKline car park.

People who never saw the station may be unable to imagine it and even those who did see it may not be able to remember it in detail.

Perhaps this book will help.

The station and the fields are just one example of many features that have changed within living memory. Nineteenth century factories and schools have either been demolished to make way for green spaces and new houses, or have survived and been turned into flats.

The town has a history of nearly nine hundred years, so inevitably much has changed and much has disappeared, but the remains of the castle can still be seen. The plan of the main streets can be traced back to ancient times, though the streets are lined with buildings from many different periods.

Just as photographs of buildings show changes in the town itself, pictures of people show changes in how they dressed and what they did. Boys no longer wear formal jackets in infant schools, and ladies no longer feel that they are required to wear hats on formal occasions. The once popular operatic society no longer exists and the cycling club shown in this book has now disbanded.

The pages that follow tell stories of a constantly changing town.

Mr. Alan Wilkinson
Local Historian

The castle ruins still stand, but Ullathorne's Mill has gone, demolished in 1976. The gas works (on the left of this picture) have also disappeared, having lasted for about 150 years. It began production in 1835.

THE TEES AT BARNARD CASTLE

In the foreground is the broken dam (or 'the warrens', as it is called locally). It was built to divert part of the Tees in order to drive the machinery in Ullathorne's Mill, which can be seen to the right of the Bridge.

This open grassy area beside the Tees was given the name 'The Bandstand' because in the early 20th Century bands played there on Sunday afternoons (there was never a constructed bandstand). The photograph is dated 1960. Nowadays the view of the river is obscured by self-seeded trees.

View looking along the River Tees towards the County Bridge c.1900.

COUNTY BRIDGE, BARNARD CASTLE. (5)

View of the County Bridge c.1890. The houses beneath the castle walls have long since been demolished.

View of The Bank, c.1900, looking towards Blagraves House in the centre of the photograph.

A quiet afternoon in the Market Place c.1870. The entrance to Newgate was very narrow. On the left hand corner stood The Queen's Head (part of the site now occupied by Barclays Bank) and to the right were two shops which were demolished in 1933-4.

THE BUTTERMARKET, BARNARD CASTLE

Modern photograph of the Buttermarket/Market Cross looking towards the Market Place c.1970.

The Market Place on market day c.1930 - a scene that has changed little over many years.

KINGS HEAD HOTEL & MARKET CROSS, BARNARD CASTLE.

Looking towards the Buttermarket/Market Cross c.1930, with the King's Head Hotel to the right of the photograph.

A busy market day looking towards Horsemarket and Galgate c.1915.

A Horse Fair was held in Galgate until World War II began in 1939. It was held just opposite Thompson & Foster's butchers shop. The young gentleman, with the bare knees, went on to become a butcher himself, Bill Peat.

Market day in Galgate c.1900. This photograph was taken from the first floor of Addisons the estate agents, by either J T Bainbridge or Elijah Yeoman.

View looking up Galgate c.1900. The Commercial Hotel is in the middle left of the photograph.

Cattle being taken up Galgate from the auction mart to the goods station, a common sight in the 1930s. The railings round the grass enclosures were removed for other uses during World War II.

This was the Wesleyan School, which opened in 1839. It was known to a later generation as The 'Council School' when it was run by Durham County Council. Houses now stand on the site.

The Primitive Methodist Church in Newgate, shortly before it was demolished to make way for a block of flats which opened in 1992.

The owner of this shop in Horsemarket (today the Victoria Wine shop) was taken to court by the local Council about issues relating to the ownership and use of his shop doorway. The Council eventually lost the case. One morning, a gun (part of the Galgate Memorial) and a notice appeared outside the shop. Mr. Harris (the shop owner) responded to the notice which said 'surrender or die' by inscribing the words 'no surrender' on his shop window. This earned him the nickname 'no surrender Harris'.

Dobson's Tripe Shop in Bridgegate c.1900, probably the last thatched roof in the town.

Photograph of Blagraves House c.1900, where Oliver Cromwell is reported to have stayed when visiting the town. It is now a restaurant.

Bridgegate Co-op shop and staff in the 1920's.

Barnard Castle's passenger station stood on what is now GlaxoSmithKline car park. A train is leaving the main platform for Darlington. The line closed for passengers in 1964.

A train arriving from Darlington. Barnard Castle Station was owned by the London North Eastern Railway, but the trucks on the left are from the London, Midland and Scottish Railway, and the Southern Railway. The actual goods station was near the Galgate end of Montalbo Road.

Deepdale Viaduct was crossed by trains going between Barnard Castle and areas west of the Pennines via the Stainmore line. The highest passenger line in England, it was closed in 1962 and the viaduct was demolished the following year.

The Tees Viaduct being reinforced during World War I to enable heavier trains to be carried. Glasgow riveters were employed, and two stayed in the town resulting in the names McGreehin and Tavendale becoming Barnard Castle names.

The opening of the bandstand in the Bowes Museum park, 1912. The bandstand replaced an ornamental lake which had been there originally; now the bandstand has gone and the lake has been restored.

Deerbolt Camp field, before there were any permanent buildings on it. This military parade which assembled there was part of Queen Victoria's Diamond Jubilee celebrations in 1897. Very little of the western part of the town had been built at that time.

King Edward VII being driven over the County Bridge in 1907. From time to time he visited upper Teesdale for the shooting.

The annual 'Meet' was originally a cyclists meet, where cycling clubs decorated the public houses which were their temporary headquarters. Here, one of Barnard Castle's two clubs has decorated The Boars Head, at the top of The Bank, to look like the rocks and water of High Force. Photograph taken c.1920.

Laying the foundation stone of the new Parish Hall in Newgate c.1950. The Vicar, the Rev. Alan Webster, was largely responsible for the idea of the new hall.

Egglestone Abbey and an open air service, possibly a service of remembrance c.1914-18.

A photograph taken in the Market Place on the day the Bowes Museum opened. 10th June 1892.

Peace Procession, Galgate 1919.

The Cyclists Meet on an outing to the Abbey Bridge. The dresses and hats would suggest it was just before the First World War. The traffic being held up is horse drawn, imagine the fuss that would have been made today!

Whit Sunday, Sunday School procession c.1910.

The unveiling of Boer War Memorial, Galgate c.1905 approx.

One of the mill chimneys being dropped into the river c.1933. The local Scouts, who just happened to need a new hut, later went into the river, fished out the bricks, then hauled them up to the new hut site in Wilson Street.

Barnard Castle mart during its centenary year 1992.

There were three boys troops in the town. A Boys Brigade, now disbanded, a Scout troop, still going strong and shown here, The Church Lads Brigade, also now disbanded. They are shown here on parade for the photo call c.1940, with the Vicar, the Rev. B. Selwyn Smith, on the Vicarage lawn.

Woodleigh men filling sandbags, 1940.

This photo marking the retirement of Post mistress, Miss Monkhouse was taken by Elijah Yeoman, the Barnard Castle photographer c.1880. The post office is now Ascough's toy shop.

Two members of the Howson family, on leave together c.1940. Note, one is wearing a WW1 uniform.

North East Quilting Class, Barnard Castle late 1930's. The gentleman on the left is Maurice Woodhams. He spent his life with his legs in callipers, which at that time would have prevented him from taking part in many activities. However, it didn't stop him from playing table tennis and cricket, shoemaking, and as seen here, quilting.

Children from the Church of England infants department are in The Bowes Museum Park at a rehearsal for celebrating the Silver Jubilee of King George V and Queen Mary in 1935. The boys from left to right are: Eric Shortridge, Jackie Lodge, Eric Hardy, Alan Wilkinson, Denis Ascough, David Parkinson, Cyril Young, and Jack Hatton. The teacher is Miss Hyslop.

Barnard Castle Church of England School girls class 1922. The gentleman to the left is the School Attendance Officer, better known as the 'Kiddy Catcher'. His name was Captain Higginbotham.

There were a number of small private schools in the town. The one run by Miss Eglinton was held at 30 Bede Road, and was inevitably known as 'Eggies'. A few of these children lived to see the 21st Century.

Barnard Castle Church of England School Junior Cricket Team c.1930.

Skating on the Tees below the aqueduct, 1940.

A ladies cricket team at a sports day held on the town cricket field c.1948. They played against gentlemen from the Town Team who were required to play left handed.

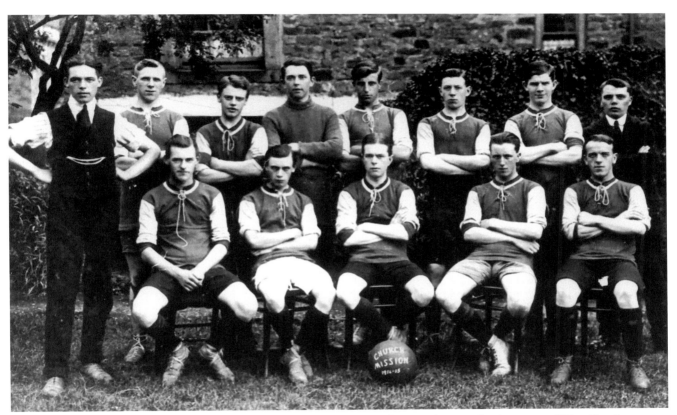

St. Mary's Mission football team, 1914-15. The mission was located near the bottom of The Bank.

Part of the chorus of 'Ruddigore' by Gilbert and Sullivan, produced by Barnard Castle Operatic Society in 1926, in the Victoria Hall in Birch Road. The producer and stage manager are also present.

Part of the cast of 'The Heiress', a play based on Henry James' novel 'Washington Square'. It was produced in the early 1950s by the Drama Section of the Amateur Operatic and Dramatic Society, on the stage of the Victoria Hall. Left to Right: Arnold Snodgrass, Joyce Plews, Denis Pickering, Alan Wilkinson, Dorothy Shanks, Mary Snodgrass (in front) and Jean Knight.

Trial by Jury in the Victoria Hall in 1908. This production led to the formation of The Barnard Castle Operatic and Drama Society and their first production was of HMS Pinafore in 1911.

A 1949 production of Merrie England performed in The Bowes Museum Park by the Barnard Castle Musical Pageant Society, the inspiration of the Rotary Club. Two hundred pounds was raised to help support The Bowes Museum. Shortly afterwards, The Friends of the Bowes Museum was founded and it still continues its good work today.

St Mary's Church Youth Dance Team, 1956.

Barnard Castle Amateur Operatic Society. The first production after World War II was 'Miss Hook of Holland'.

Acknowledgments:

Durham County Council would like to thank the following for kindly providing photographs reproduced in this book.

Mr. Parkin Raine
The Bowes Museum - permission given to Mr. Raine to use the images
Mr. Alan Wilkinson
Mr. Alan Wright.

Our thanks also go to Mr. Alan Wilkinson, (local historian - author of several books about Barnard Castle) for writing the introduction to this book.

A special mention must be given to Barnard Castle Library staff, whose in-depth local knowledge helped identify many of the photographs.